To Callum on your 9th birthday.

Love from Rhona.

To Callum on your 9th birthday.

Love from Rhona.

THE BIG BOOK OF

EXPLORERS

DAVID MARSHALL

HAMLYN

The Big Book of Explorers was
produced for Hamlyn Children's Books
by Lionheart Books, London

Published in 1992 by
Hamlyn Children's Books.
part of Reed International Books.
Michelin House, 81 Fulham Road.
London SW3 6RB

ISBN 0 600 57364 8

Printed in Italy

CONTENTS

THE FIRST EXPLORERS

Exploration is one of the oldest and most exciting human activities. Some explorers have been driven by curiosity, some by a desire to spread a religion or to discover riches, and others by the need to find a refuge or new home.

Although the reasons for their journeys may differ, all explorers share special qualities. These are, above all, the love of adventure and the desire to discover the unknown. Many explorers have been willing to face ridicule, danger, and even death to achieve their goals. Today the spirit of adventure, and the urge to expand human knowledge, live on in space exploration and the quest for scientific knowledge.

EARLY SETTLERS AND TRADERS

The earliest explorers lived about 40,000 years ago. They were Stone Age hunters who travelled through strange and alien lands in search of food. About 20,000 years ago came the Stone Age villagers, who kept herds of animals and grew the first crops. They had a poorer diet than the hunters, and suffered more from disease, but they also bred more children. Once their primitive farming methods had exhausted the soil, and they could no longer feed their bigger families, they had to move on and explore new areas.

Perhaps the first explorers in the true sense were traders from countries in the ancient Near East, like Assyria, Babylonia, and Egypt. Probably the earliest named explorer was an Egyptian called Hennu. In about 2500 B.C. he and his companions crossed the desert to the Red Sea. Here they built boats and sailed down the Red Sea to Punt, on Africa's east coast, near what is now Somalia. Hennu loaded his ship with gold, ivory and myrrh and took them back to Egypt.

Below: To survive, early peoples had to explore. They cut down trees and lashed them together to make the first boats, or rafts. Later, they learned how to hollow out huge tree trunks to make canoes, and to inflate animal skins under the rafts to make them float better.

Right: An Assyrian riverboat as shown on stone from a palace at Nineveh, Assyria. Assyria and Babylonia were civilizations from about 2000 to 500 B.C. in what is now Iraq. The early Assyrian ships were biremes, meaning "two rows of oars." In these ships Babylonian trading expeditions travelled as far west as the Mediterranean Sea, and as far south as the Indian Ocean.

ANCIENT SEA-FARERS

Ancient Egypt was centred on the banks of the River Nile, its territory stretching in length for more than 1,600 km. The Egyptians became great experts at boat-building. There are wall paintings from as early as about 2800 B.C. showing them building boats. It was only natural that they would begin to explore further afield. Before long, they had become aware of, and sailed around the Mediterranean Sea. By 1700 B.C. – when the wheel was first introduced into Egypt – the Egyptians had been exploring by sea for more than 1,000 years.

The small island of Crete in the Mediterranean, where the land was very fertile, was home to the Minoans. They too were a sea-faring people, who before 1500 B.C. had sent ships as far as Sicily. However, by far the greatest explorers of ancient times were the

Above: Egyptian traders, sent to Punt by Queen Hatshepsut in 1500 B.C. return in their ships, with herbs and spices.

Phoenicians. The Phoenicians lived at the eastern end of the Mediterranean in the coastal areas of what are now Israel, Lebanon, and Syria. Perhaps as early as 1100 B.C., Phoenician sailors became the first to sail the length of the Mediterranean Sea. In about 750 B.C. they established Carthage, near present-day Tunis. Later they sailed through the Straits of Gibraltar to explore the Atlantic coast of North Africa.

Although not a true explorer, the Carthaginian general Hannibal (247-183 B.C.) went where no army had been before – and took his elephants with him! Carthage and Rome were at war and Hannibal wanted to surprise the enemy. Setting out from Spain, he marched his elephants across southern France to the River Rhône. From there he went north to confuse the Romans. Then he turned round, crossed the Alps, and attacked.

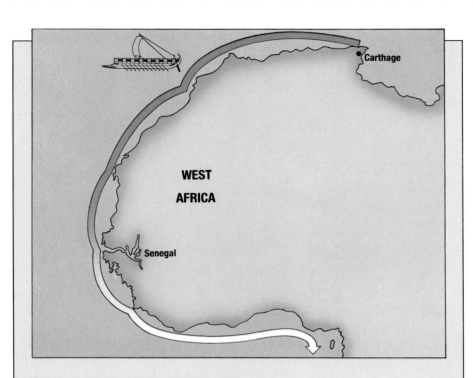

Phoenician explorations 500 to 400 B.C.

Hanno, a Carthaginian navigator who lived from about 490 to 420 B.C., commanded a fleet of 60 ships, sent out to establish settlements on the African coast. He probably reached as far south as present-day Senegal before running short of food and returning home. In Morocco, he founded the cities of Mogador and Agadir, and in west Africa he saw crocodiles and hippopotamuses.

Left: It must have been both terrifying and amazing for the natives of African countries along the Nile and the Red Sea to see the arrival of the huge Egyptian ships. Their world was being invaded and it would never be the same again. True exploration had begun.

THE GREEKS AND ROMANS

The Ancient Greeks learned more about the world than any other people before them. In the fifth and fourth centuries B.C. Hippocrates founded modern medicine, Euclid created modern mathematics, and Plato and Aristotle founded modern philosophy. Meanwhile, Greek sailors explored the Mediterranean coasts of Europe and Africa looking for places to colonize. Two of the most important of these explorers were Pytheas, an astronomer, and Alexander the Great, a king, general and conqueror.

Pytheas lived in Massalia, which was then occupied by Greece. (Today it is called Marseilles, and is in southern France). In the fourth century B.C. Pytheas sailed from Massalia through the Straits of Gibraltar. He explored the Atlantic coasts of what are now Portugal, Spain and France. Sailing north he passed the British Isles and did not stop until ice blocked his way and forced him to turn back.

At about the same time, Alexander the Great, the son of the King of Macedonia (a country forming part of modern Greece) began an amazing journey of conquest. In 333 B.C. Alexander, then aged 22, and his army of 35,000 soldiers defeated a Persian army in what is now Turkey. They marched on into the Middle East and fought their way across western Asia. They conquered Babylonia, Persia and much of Afghanistan before reaching India and turning back. Alexander sailed down the Indus River to the Indian Ocean. On his return to the Middle East he marched westward across the Gedrosia desert in Persia.

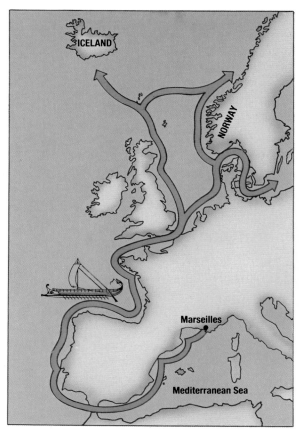

Left: Pytheas spoke of a land called Ultima Thule, which was the northernmost point of his journey. Today experts think he had reached Iceland or Norway.

Right: A fifteenth-century map based on the work of Ptolemy, 100-178 A.D., an Egyptian astronomer and geographer. His books on geography were a standard source of information for European explorers until the sixteenth century.

Below: A Greek merchant vessel was sturdy and wide with a single mast bearing a square or oval sail. It was steered, and often propelled, by large oars at the stern or rear of the boat.

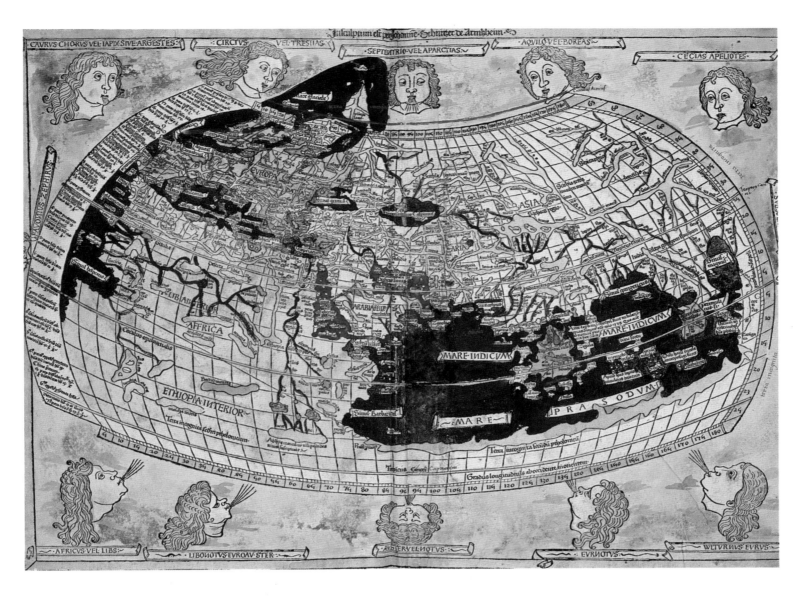

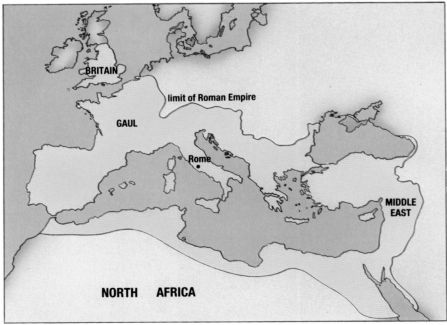

Left: At its greatest extent, from about 50 B.C. to A.D. 100, and through conquests and trade, the Roman Empire covered most of Europe and parts of North Africa, Asia and the Middle East.

Unlike the Greeks, the Romans were not great explorers. However, they did conquer lands that were little-known to them before – Britain, France, Germany, Spain – and they brought back goods from India, China and Africa. Trading with Rome increased these lands' knowledge of far-off places. The trade was continued until about A.D. 400. By that time, the Roman Empire had been overthrown by Germanic people, who had little interest in Eastern products, or exploration.

THE VIKINGS

Between A.D. 700 and 800 the people of Scandinavia began to feel the effects of many years of rapid growth in population. They became desperate to find new places to settle – and so they explored, by sailing to England, Iceland, Ireland, and Scotland.

In about A.D. 982 Eric "the Red", originally from Jaeren in southern Norway, set sail from Iceland in search of new territory. He explored the waters west of Iceland, looking for the land that another Norwegian explorer, Gunnbjorn Ulfsson, had sighted in about A.D. 900. Eric reached the huge island now known as Greenland and settled there. A few years later, the Viking captain Bjarin Herjulfsson headed for Greenland to join Eric's colony. But a storm blew him off course to the east coast of Canada. He was the first known European to see the mainland of North America. It is believed he sighted Sandwich Bay on the coast of Labrador, and Frobisher Bay at the southern end of Baffin Island.

Right: Viking settlers in Greenland around A.D. 1000. Recently archaeologists have found evidence of Viking settlements along much of the northeastern coast of North America.

Right: In little over 200 years the Vikings visited every coast in Europe. They colonized Britain and northern France, traded with the Russians, landed in Spain, North Africa, and Italy, and even reached North America. Some Viking warriors served in the Imperial Guard at Constantinople, present-day Istanbul in Turkey. The map shows the Viking's major sea routes and destinations.

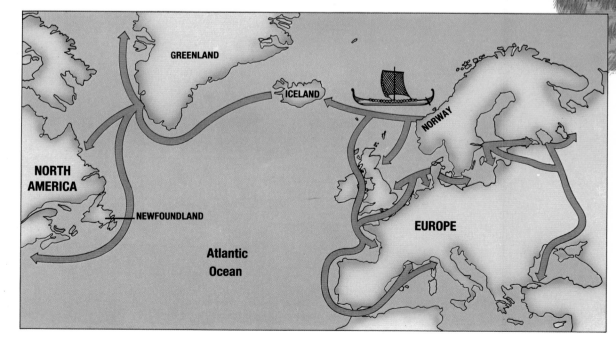

GREENLAND

ICELAND

NORWAY

NORTH AMERICA

NEWFOUNDLAND

EUROPE

Atlantic Ocean

ERIC "THE RED'S" SON
Leif Ericson was the son of Eric. Having gone with his father to Greenland, in A.D. 998 he sailed to Iceland and then to Norway. Here he became a Christian and returned to Greenland to preach at his father's settlement.

In A.D. 1000, Leif led an expedition to explore the land that Herjulfsson had reported seeing. The Vikings set up a settlement there at a place that Ericson named Vinland (Wineland) because they made wine from the local grapes. People now think these were not, in fact, grapes but cranberries or gooseberries. Nobody really knows where Vinland was, but it was no doubt the island of Newfoundland, in what is today Canada.

The Viking settlers were constantly attacked by Indians or Eskimos, and so they left Vinland, went home, and lost interest in resettling away from Europe.

Right: Viking houses, like this one at L'Anse aux Meadows, on Newfoundland, were strongly built of stone, earth and wood.

MARCO POLO

The great explorer Marco Polo was born in Venice in 1254. When he was young, he used to listen with avid interest to the stories told by his father and uncle on their return from their travels along The Great Silk Road from Europe to the Orient. In 1271, at the age of 17, Marco eagerly accompanied them back to China.

The rulers of this huge part of the world were the Mongols, led by their famous emperor Kublai Khan. He welcomed and encouraged travellers and traders, and in 1275 Marco Polo visited him in his capital city, Khanbalik – today's Beijing. The great Khan made Marco one of the senior foreign officials at his court in order to keep him in China. For nearly 20 years, Marco, his father and uncle, traded, travelled, and explored throughout all China.

By 1292 the Polos were very wealthy and were keen to return home. Their chance came when

Above: A sixteenth-century painting of Venice, Italy, as it was thought to look at the time that Marco, his father, and uncle set out in 1271 on a voyage which lasted 25 years.

Right: Marco Polo and his father approach a walled town in China just as a trading caravan is arriving.

Kublai Khan needed someone to escort a young princess on her journey from China to Persia. He asked the Polos to look after her.

Returning by the ocean route, to avoid the wars that were being fought on land, Marco traded with many peoples and recorded his impressions of the exciting places that he visited. He spoke later of the island of Ceylon, today's Sri Lanka, and his voyage end in Hormuz in the Persian Gulf. After Marco Polo, no European travelled this way again for many years.

The adventures of Marco Polo only became known to the world by accident. During a naval battle he was captured by the Genoese. In prison in Genoa, he told his story to a writer, Rusticiano of Pisa, who was captured with him. Rusticiano wrote down his story, calling it *The Travels of Marco Polo*. At the time, hardly any of it was believed, but in the last 600 years much of what Marco Polo wrote has proved to be true. This book also caught the imagination of others in later years, including Christopher Columbus.

Right: The travels and trading journeys of Nicolo Polo and later, of his son, Marco Polo. Marco was the only European to explore China during the thirteenth century and until Dutch, French and English traders arrived in the seventeenth century.

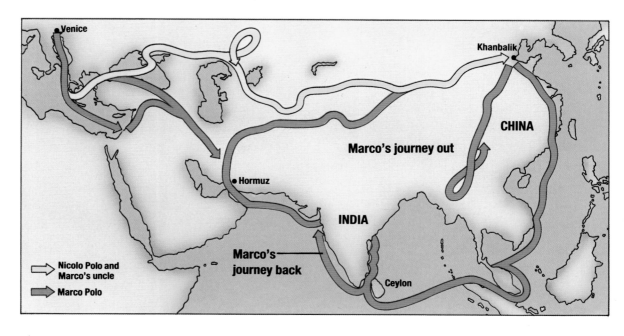

IBN BATUTA

The fourteenth-century explorer Ibn Batuta was a Muslim who came from a wealthy family in Tangier, Morocco. When he was 21, he travelled to Mecca, on a *Haji* (pilgrimage) that all good Muslims try to make at least once in their lifetime. On the way, he stayed the night in Alexandria, Egypt, and had a strange dream. He dreamt that he travelled on the wing of a huge bird all over the known Muslim world, and beyond. A Muslim holy man explained the dream, telling Ibn Batuta that he would spend the rest of his life travelling through Asia – and that is what he did!

A Muslim scholar, Ibn Batuta visited many Islamic holy places and was accepted everywhere as a great man. Princes, princesses, and governors greeted him and often showered him with gifts and honours. In the Maldive Islands in India, he became a judge. He so impressed the Sultan of Delhi that he was sent as the Sultan's special ambassador to China in 1342.

However, the way he lived exposed him to great danger. While travelling from India to China he was captured by Hindus, who stripped and robbed him, leaving him to wander for eight days alone before he rejoined his companions. He was also at risk from disease. In 1349 he visited Syria at the time when 2,400 people were dying every day from the Black Death.

Ibn Batuta spent over 30 years travelling. He covered some 200,000 km visiting every Islamic country. On his return to Morocco, the Sultan ordered one of his secretaries to write down Ibn's story. That is how today we have a record of most of his travels.

Left: A detail of the Catalan Atlas of the World of 1375 which showed European merchants on their journey overland to China as well as Ibn Batuta on his travels by camel.

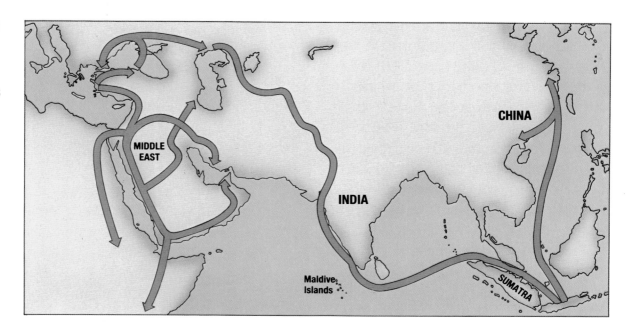

Below: An illustration from fourteenth-century writer Rashid al-Din's *World History* showing Muslim travellers on a *haji*. Like Ibn Batuta, they journeyed on camels.

Above: Ibn Batuta, between about 1320 and 1354, travelled throughout the Muslim world from Africa to China and Sumatra in the Far East.

PRINCE HENRY THE NAVIGATOR

Prince Henry was the third son of John I of Portugal and Philippa of Lancaster. In 1415 he, along with his two older brothers, captured the Moroccan town of Ceuta for the Portuguese. The commercial routes between Ceuta and central Africa fascinated Henry and he began to organize expeditions along the northwest African coast.

One of Henry's goals was to send explorers beyond Cape Bojador on the west coast of Africa – the most westerly point known to Europeans at that time. After several unsuccessful attempts, one of Henry's explorers, Gil Eaures, passed the Cape in 1434. Another, Antao Goncalves, returned to Portugal in 1441 with some Africans he had captured. These people were the first slaves brought from West Africa to Europe. Among them was a chief, called Adahu, who told Henry about lands further south and inland. To investigate, Nuno Tristao, in 1441, sailed as far south as Cape Blanc, on the border of Western Sahara and Mauritania. Four years later, Diniz Diaz reached Cape Verde, Senegal. By the time of Henry's death, in 1460, Portuguese ships had reached the coast of Sierra Leone.

Although usually called "The Navigator", Henry did not go on expeditions himself, but planned and raised the money for others to do so in more than 50 missions. The navigational knowledge gained under Henry's direction led to several historic voyages within 50 years of his death. They included the voyages of Vasco da Gama and Bartholomew Diaz around the southern tip of Africa.

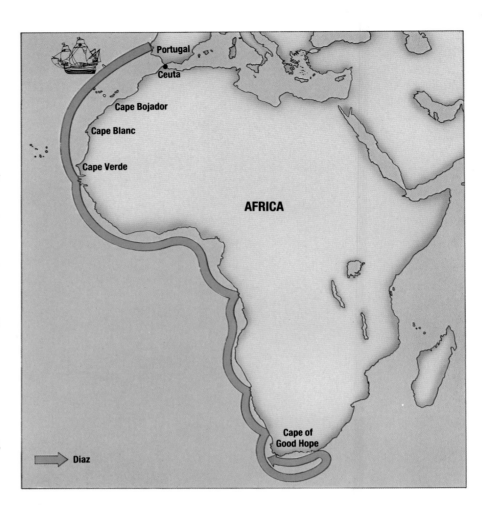

Above: Henry's expeditions went south, further and further along the African coast, and into the interior.

Below: A huge cross marking the spot where Portuguese explorers, sent out by Prince Henry, landed. Religion was important to many of them and they wanted to convert the inhabitants of newly discovered lands to Christianity.

Above: Henry "the Navigator", whose vision, industry and wealth laid the foundations of the great Portuguese overseas empire that flourished during the sixteenth and seventeenth centuries.

CHENG HO

In 1405 an expedition greater than any attemped in Europe before that time set sail from the harbour of Nanking in China. It included 63 huge treasure ships and 250 smaller vessels, which together carried almost 28,000 men on board. The commander of the fleet was Cheng Ho, who had been chosen by the Ming Emperor of China, Yung Lo, to lead the expedition because he was a great soldier. The emperor's faith in him was justified, as Cheng also became a great sailor and trader. The ships in Cheng's fleet were junks, a type that is still in use, except that today's junks are much smaller. An enormous rudder post found by archaeologists in Nanking in 1962, proved that some of Cheng's junks must have been 160 m long!

As well as the crew, the ships carried a large number of passengers. There were doctors, soldiers, bankers, merchants, translators, clerks, boat repairers, priests, and – to make friends with people from other countries – diplomats. There was also cargo. Wherever he visited, Cheng Ho took gifts of tea, silk, and porcelain, and he returned to China with overseas visitors and their gifts. He was particularly popular when he brought back exotic animals such as giraffes, lions, and ostriches. Unfortunately not everyone believed in exploration, and all of Cheng's journals from his travels were destroyed by jealous court officials.

Above: Cheng Ho sailing off the African coast. The ships he used – junks – had a flat bottom and squarish sails. The expedition of 1405 was the first of seven that Cheng Ho led up to 1433, visiting over 30 countries.

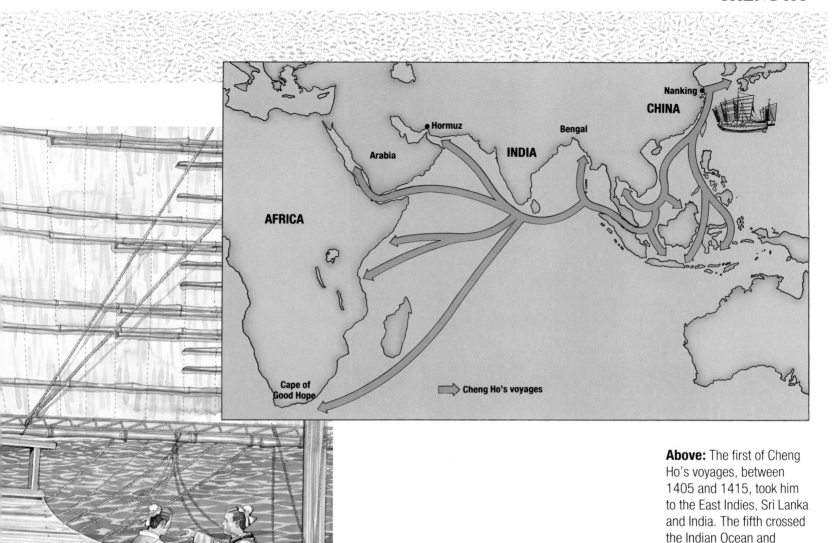

Above: The first of Cheng Ho's voyages, between 1405 and 1415, took him to the East Indies, Sri Lanka and India. The fifth crossed the Indian Ocean and reached Hormuz and the east coast of Africa. On the sixth voyage one of Cheng's junks visited Bengal, and on the seventh Arabia.

No one really knows why the Chinese suddenly started these amazing voyages of discovery – or why they stopped just as suddenly. Maybe the voyages became too expensive – for little gain. Perhaps the Emperor Yung Lo had a personal interest in exploration, and on his death in 1424 most of the interest died too. After that, Cheng Ho only went on one more journey – and later no one followed his example.

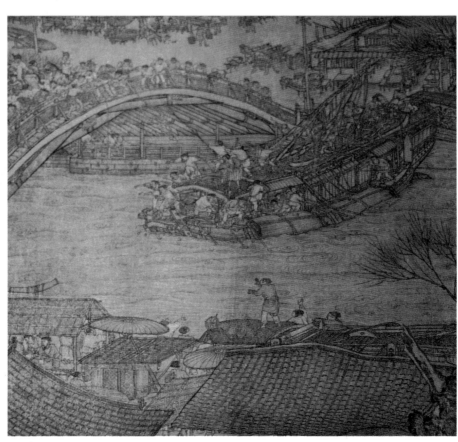

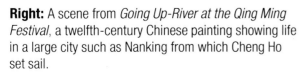

Right: A scene from *Going Up-River at the Qing Ming Festival*, a twelfth-century Chinese painting showing life in a large city such as Nanking from which Cheng Ho set sail.

CHRISTOPHER COLUMBUS

Christopher Columbus was born in Genoa in Italy, but settled in Portugal in 1478. As a youth, he desperately wanted to be a sailor, after his father sent him on a trading mission. He read the *Travels of Marco Polo* and dreamed of sailing west to reach the east. In the East were spices, which at the time were worth more than gold. Anyone who could bring them to Europe by a better route than overland through Asia would become rich.

Columbus loved the idea of exploration and discovery for its own sake, but he also wanted wealth and honours. After many attempts, he persuaded King Ferdinand and Queen Isabella of Spain to pay for his first expedition.

In August 1492, Columbus left Palos in Spain on his first trip to the "East", which led to his discovery of The New World. After a voyage full of incidents including a near-mutiny, he reached his destination on 12th October. He probably landed on the island of Samana Cay, which he named San Salvador, meaning "The Saviour". He thought that he was in the East Indies, and called the natives Indians. During this first trip he also discovered Cuba and Haiti. On his return to Spain in March 1493, he was greatly honoured. He had achieved his ambition of becoming a rich and important man.

Columbus's second voyage, between 1493 and 1496, led to the discovery of Guadeloupe, Antigua, Montserrat, Puerto Rico, and Jamaica. During the third voyage, in 1498, he came across Trinidad and though he did not realize it, the South American mainland.

Below: *"Tierra! Tierra!"*, the welcome cry from the lookout on 12th October 1492 announced that land had been sighted at last. The men were safe and Columbus had found the "New World".

After failing to conquer the people of these lands, he was sent back to Spain in chains in the year 1500. The King and Queen forgave him, but the experience left him bitter. He led one last voyage, between 1502 and 1504, which he paid for himself. He and his crew explored the coast of Honduras and Nicaragua. In 1506 a sad Columbus died penniless in Valladolid, Spain. He was buried in Seville cathedral.

Between 1499 and 1504 an Italian, Amerigo Vespucci, led three voyages to South America. He claimed he had reached the "New World". In 1507, a German map-maker, Waldseemuller, suggested the New World be named America, after Amerigo Vespucci.

Below: The routes of Columbus's four voyages of discovery to the New World. He believed that a route to the East lay beyond the islands.

N. AMERICA — Atlantic Ocean — PORTUGAL — SPAIN — AFRICA — S. AMERICA

→ 1st voyage
→ 2nd voyage
→ 3rd voyage
→ 4th voyage

Right: Columbus lands at Samana Cay and is greeted by the "Indians". In the words of someone living at the time, Columbus was a "well-built man of more than average height. His face was long with rather high cheek bones; his person neither fat nor thin. He had a hooked nose, light eyes and a fair skin with a ruddy tinge."

ROUNDING THE CAPE

In 1487 King John II of Portugal ordered Bartholomew Diaz to sail to the Cape of Good Hope at the southern end of Africa. The King wanted to know if ships could sail to Asia around Africa. Others had tried before but had failed.

Diaz set off in the summer of 1487 with three ships. Sailing down the coast of Africa, they met with terrible storms, which blew them out to sea for 13 days. When, at last, they sighted land, Diaz realized that he had rounded the Cape. Now in the Indian Ocean, he wanted to sail along the coast to India but his men persuaded him to go back. On the return voyage, he sighted the Cape of Good Hope. He arrived back in December 1488.

Right: Vasco da Gama. His voyage around Africa was of great importance, because the Turks had blocked the land routes from India to Europe along which spices and other riches were transported.

Navigation

By the end of the fifteenth century, European mariners were able to follow set courses using instruments such as the compass and astrolabe. A type of compass using lodestone was invented by the Chinese perhaps 2,000 years ago, and the present-day version was brought to Europe from China by Arab traders around A.D. 1200. The Astrolobe is used to find the height above the horizon of the Sun or a bright star.

Above: A ship's navigator using an astrolabe to measure latitude. He points the sighting arm towards the Sun or a bright star such as the Pole Star, and reads off the angle from a scale on the disc. At the North Pole a small adjustment is needed to obtain a true reading.

In 1494 Diaz directed the building of two of the three ships intended for another expedition around the Cape, this time all the way to India. Under the command of Vasco da Gama, the three ships, with 170 men on board, rounded the Cape on 22nd November. The expedition was important because of the different route that da Gama had taken. He had sailed away from the African coast, and almost over to Brazil, in order to pick up favourable winds that would carry him past the dreaded Cape. This became the standard route for centuries after. Da Gama stopped at African trading centres on his way to India, which he reached on 20th May 1498.

The Muslim merchants who controlled trade in India hated the Portuguese and so da Gama did not make his fortune there. Bartholomew Diaz was even less fortunate. In 1500 he tried to follow da Gama's course but ran aground in heavy seas in Brazil. On his way back to Portugal he drowned when his ship sank in a storm.

Da Gama returned to India in 1502 to establish Portuguese rule and expand his country's trade. Using ruthless and cruel methods he succeeded in both. As a reward for his success, da Gama went to Portugal to be made Viceroy of India by King John III in 1524. He returned to India in that same year and died shortly afterwards.

Right: As well as Diaz and da Gama, other Portuguese explorers were important in mapping the world and expanding King John II's empire. Pedro Cabral discovered Brazil, Pedro de Covilhao visited Ethiopia and prepared the way for da Gama, and Afonso de Albuquerque as Governor-General of India seized and colonized Goa, Malacca, and the coast of Ceylon.

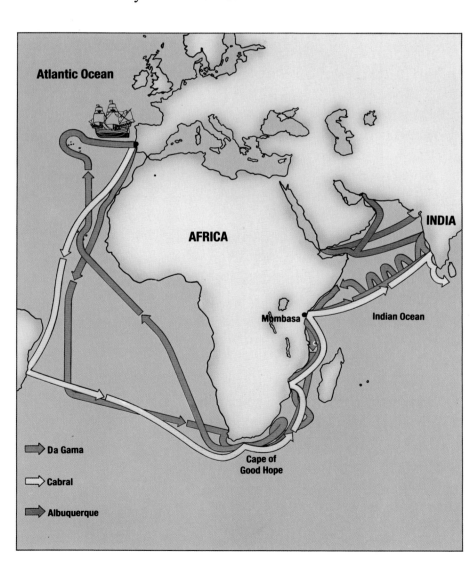

Atlantic Ocean

AFRICA

INDIA

Mombasa

Indian Ocean

Cape of Good Hope

Da Gama

Cabral

Albuquerque

TO THE AMERICAS

In 1497 Henry VII of England was told by a Genoese, John Cabot, that, by going north, Columbus's Indies (the American continent) – and valuable spices – could be reached by a much shorter route than Columbus had taken. Cabot proved that he was right. He set sail from Bristol, and after about a month landed in Canada.

Some 10 years later the English King sent Sebastian Cabot, John's son, to look for a water route through the land area discovered by his father. Thus began the search for the Northwest Passage. Sebastian's quest took him as far south as the present-day state of North Carolina. In 1513 a Spaniard, Vasco Nunez de Balboa, led an expedition across Panama from the Atlantic to the Pacific coast. He was the first European to see the Pacific Ocean and so proved that the "New World" was a huge land- mass between Europe and Asia.

Another Spaniard, Hernando Cortes, sailed with about 600 men, in 1519, from Cuba to the east coast of what is now Mexico. Hearing that Aztec Indians ruled a great civilization some distance inland, he marched his army to Tenochtitlan (now Mexico City) and conquered the Aztecs. In 1533, Francisco Pizarro conquered and destroyed the wealthy empire of the Inca Indians in Peru.

In 1513 Juan Ponce de Leon sailed from Puerto Rico in search of gold and landed on the east coast of Florida. He was followed in 1539 by an army of about 600 Spaniards, commanded by Hernando de Soto, who arrived on the west coast of Florida. They travelled far and wide but found no gold.

Pizarro

Left: Francisco Pizarro. He led a small force of Spanish adventurers who overthrew the Inca empire in Peru. He also founded the city of Lima in 1535. Pedro de Mendoza took the first settlers to Argentina in 1536. He established the town of Buenos Aires. When this came under attack by Indians, the settlers abandoned it and moved inland to Ascuncion, now the capital of Paraguay.

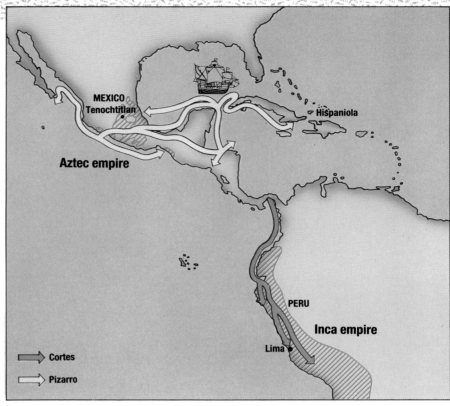

Left: Cortes's men slaughter the Aztecs in one of many bloody battles. The Aztecs believed that their god, Quetzalcoatl, had a white face and a beard, wore a high-crowned hat, and carried new weapons. When they first saw Cortes, they mistook him for Quetzalcoatl!

Above: The expeditions and explorations of the *conquistadores*, the Spanish conquerors of Mexico and Peru in the sixteenth century. From bases on the Caribbean islands, especially Hispaniola – present-day Haiti and Dominican Republic – Cortes and Pizarro led fighting forces that destroyed the Aztec and Inca empires and took their riches.

Cortes

Cartier

Left: Hernando Cortes, who led the Spaniards against the Aztecs and stole a fortune in gold and jewels from them.

Right: Jacques Cartier was a French explorer ordered by Francis I to sail in search of gold, spices, and a new route to Asia. In fact, he explored Canada, after entering the Gulf of St. Lawrence in 1534. He eventually established the first French base at Quebec and reached Montreal.

FERDINAND MAGELLAN

Below: Ship of the type that sailed with Magellan – a "nao", about 30 m long. In the autumn of 1520 Magellan's ships faced the worst weather in the world as they rounded Cape Horn and went into the Pacific Ocean.

Ferdinand Magellan became a page at the palace of Queen Leonor of Portugal at the age of 10. There he learned navigation and all about the voyages of Columbus and Vasco da Gama. He worked as a squire and clerk in a marine department, before serving in the navy in 1505 to strengthen Portuguese bases in India. In 1509 he sailed to Melaka, a commercial centre in Malaysia, where he discovered the fabulous wealth of the Spice Islands (the Moluccas).

Magellan sought the support of King Manuel I to finance a voyage west around South America to the Spice Islands, as he was certain this was a shorter route than around Africa and India. When Manuel refused to help, Magellan went to King Charles of Spain, who agreed.

On 20th September 1519 Magellan and his crew of 241 Spaniards set sail. The five ships – *Concepcion, San Antonio, Santiago, Trinidad*, and *Victoria* – sailed across the Atlantic to the coast of Brazil. After the loss of the *Santiago* during the winter, the voyage resumed from Brazil on 18th October 1520. When the crew of the *San Antonio* mutinied, only three ships were left to find the narrow passage around the tip of South America, now called the Straits of Magellan. They reached an ocean that seemed so calm that Magellan called it Pacific, meaning "peaceful".

The crews endured great hardship on the vast ocean before reaching the island of Guam in March 1521. They took enough food on board to enable them to get to the Philippines. Here they became involved in local fighting,

Above and below: Magellan's round-the-world voyage. Surprisingly, the voyage was condemned at the time. Magellan was considered a traitor by the Portuguese for using Spanish crews, while the Spanish disowned him because of his bad treatment of their men.

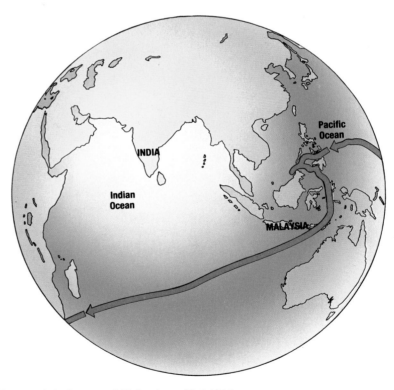

during which, on 27th April 1521, Magellan, among others, was killed. Only the *Victoria*, which sailed west around Africa, returned to Spain, arriving on 6th September 1522 – three years after the voyage began – with 18 survivors on board.

SIR FRANCIS DRAKE

Queen Elizabeth I of England encouraged her sailors to be "sea dogs" – that is, pirates who plundered the wealth of other nations for the good of her realm. The most famous of these adventurers was Sir Francis Drake.

Drake's best-known voyage began on 13th December 1577 with five ships – the *Pelican*, *Elizabeth*, and *Marigold* with 160 men on board, and the *Swan* and *Benedict* as supply vessels. Sailing west, Drake soon rounded Cape Horn through the Straits of Magellan. Here the storms were so bad that the *Marigold* was wrecked, and the *Elizabeth* was blown off course and had to return to England. Drake continued in the *Pelican*, which he renamed *The Golden Hind*.

He sailed up the Pacific coast of South America, raiding many of the Spanish ports. The Spaniards had left these unguarded as they did not expect to see other Europeans there. Drake continued north along the Pacific coast to North America to pick up supplies.

Not wishing to go south back past the Spanish ports that he had attacked, Drake sailed out into the Pacific Ocean. He entered the Indian Ocean and rounded the Cape of Good Hope without any problems. He reached Plymouth on 26th September 1580 – almost three years to go around the world.

For the rest of his life Drake continued to raid and torment the Spanish. He is held largely responsible for inciting the Spanish Armada, an invasion fleet that set sail in 1588. It was while returning from another raid on Spanish ports in the West Indies in 1595, that Drake died and was buried at sea.

Right: When Drake landed in "New Albion", just beyond what is now San Francisco, the natives thought he was a god and crowned him as their long-awaited leader. By the time he returned home, much of the New World was claimed by England.

Below: Sir Francis Drake. He was born in Plymouth, and when he was young his father became the minister at the naval shipyards at Rochester. As a young man he sailed on slave-trading expeditions with Sir John Hawkins. From 1570 to 1572 Queen Elizabeth sent him on looting missions to the West Indies.

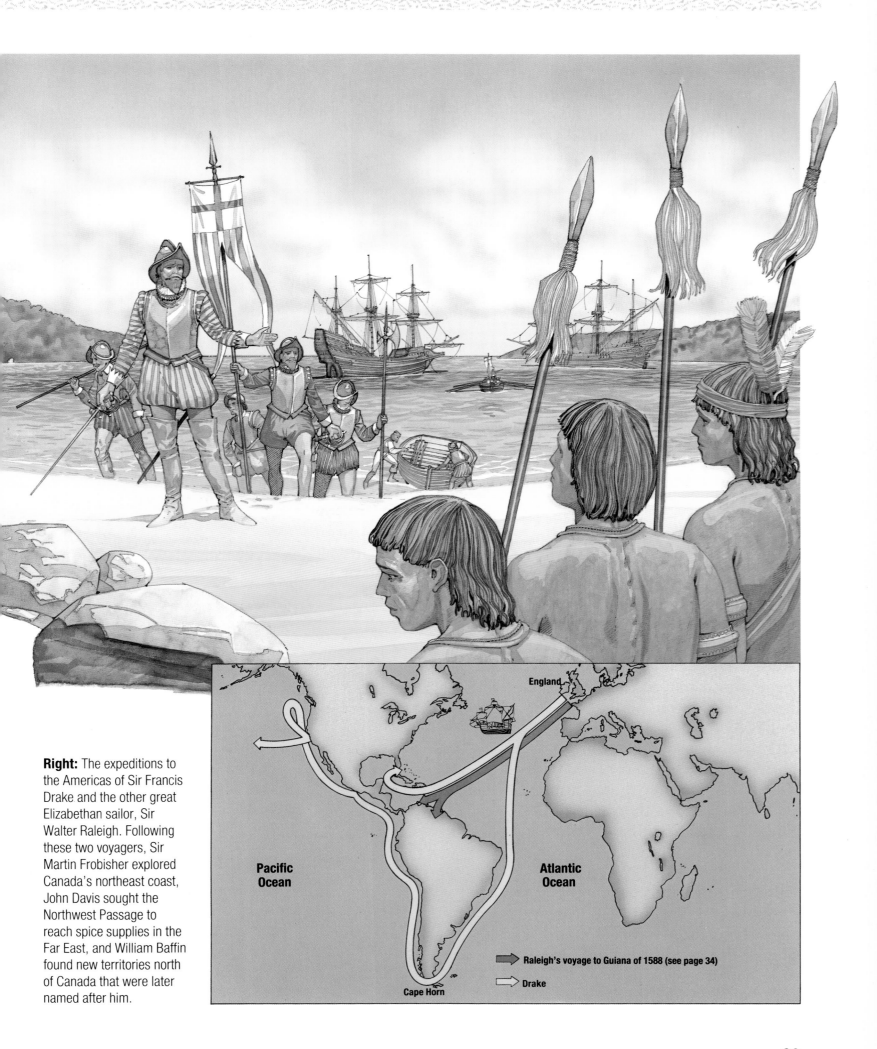

Right: The expeditions to the Americas of Sir Francis Drake and the other great Elizabethan sailor, Sir Walter Raleigh. Following these two voyagers, Sir Martin Frobisher explored Canada's northeast coast, John Davis sought the Northwest Passage to reach spice supplies in the Far East, and William Baffin found new territories north of Canada that were later named after him.

England

Pacific Ocean

Atlantic Ocean

Cape Horn

⇒ Raleigh's voyage to Guiana of 1588 (see page 34)

⇒ Drake

THE EASTERN SEABOARD

Like Sir Francis Drake, Sir Walter Raleigh was an English adventurer who lived in the reign of Queen Elizabeth I. In 1587 Raleigh took 117 settlers, including 17 women, to what is now the state of North Carolina. After exploring as far south as Florida, Raleigh named the whole region Virginia, in honour of Queen Elizabeth I, the Virgin Queen. A year later, Raleigh led an unsuccessful expedition to Guiana, in South America, to search for El Dorado, the legendary land of gold.

When James I succeeded Elizabeth, Raleigh's fortunes changed so drastically that he was imprisoned in the Tower of London with his family for 12 years. James released him to allow him to search for El Dorado again but insisted that he remain at peace with the Spanish. Raleigh refused, and attacked Spanish ships. So on his return in 1618, he was executed.

In 1606 John Smith (1579-1631), an English soldier, sailed on an expedition to establish a permanent colony in Jamestown, Virginia, where Raleigh had settled before. The colonists had to endure disease, starvation, and many attacks by Indians. From 1608 to 1609 Smith was president of the colony and he traded for food with the Indians. But they hated him because he treated them harshly. When he left, the Indians almost wiped out the colony.

Smith returned to America in 1614 to explore the coast in the Massachusetts Bay area. He named it New England. He stressed the value of fish, fur and timber for trade, but criticized useless searches for gold and silver.

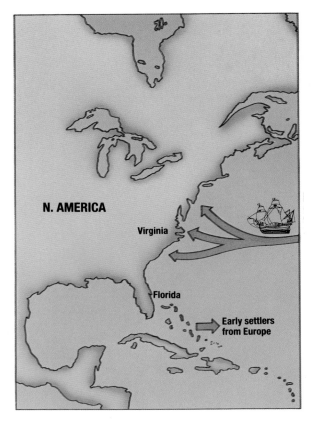

Left: The eastern seaboard of America that was colonized by Sir Walter Raleigh, John Smith and others. Many of the places along the coast are still known by the names given them at that time, such as New Hampshire, New England, and Virginia.

Below: Sir Walter Raleigh and son. The Queen was so charmed by Raleigh that she gave him an estate of 5,000 hectares and the right to colonize in America. Raleigh introduced Europe to tobacco and the potato from the New World.

Their rype corne

Their greene corne.

Corne newly sprong.

Their sitting at meate

The place of solemne prayer

The house wherin the Tombe of their Herounds standeth

SECOTON·

A Ceremony in their prayers strange iestures and songs danfs abowt posts carued on the topp lyke mens faces.

Above: The southern cabin in Raleigh's colony which, on 18th August 1587, was the birthplace of the first English child to be born in North America.

Left: The Indian village of Secoton, Virginia. The painting is by John White, leader of Raleigh's 117 settlers who tried to establish a colony along the eastern seaboard in 1587.

35

NEW FRANCE

Sir Martin Frobisher explored Canada's northeast coast and set sail with three ships in 1576 to search for a northwest passage to Asia. He reached as far as Labrador and Baffin Island. In 1585 he became vice-admiral to Drake and fought against the Spanish Armada.

Henry Hudson was another English seaman at about the same time, after whom the Hudson River, Hudson Strait and Hudson Bay are all named. He explored the islands north of Norway in search of a northeast passage to Asia. Then in 1609 he sailed up the Hudson River to find a northwest passage, in an expedition financed not by England but by the Dutch East India Company. He passed through Hudson Strait and Hudson Bay in the following year, but died a year later when his crew mutinied and abandoned him.

Samuel de Champlain was a French explorer. The son of a sea captain who taught him navigation, he made several voyages to the West Indies, Mexico, and Panama from 1599 to 1601. On his return to France, he wrote a book about his voyages, describing the splendour of Mexico City and proposing that a canal be built across Panama. This book interested the French king Henri IV, who wanted to extract wealth from North America and also hoped to find a northwest passage. Consequently, in 1603 Champlain sailed to Canada and explored the St. Lawrence River. He was one of the first Europeans to write about the Niagara Falls.

Returning to Canada in 1604, Champlain investigated the New England area and founded Port Royal in Nova Scotia.

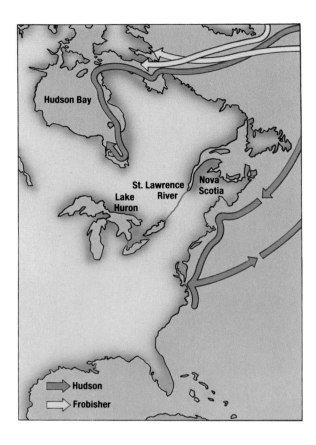

Hudson Bay

St. Lawrence River

Lake Huron

Nova Scotia

→ Hudson
⇨ Frobisher

Left: The voyages of Hudson, and Frobisher, and the Dutch explorer William Barents, opened up and established the New France. Barents, in 1596, sailed to the Arctic Ocean north of Russia looking for a way to reach East Asia. His ship became frozen in a sea of ice for the whole of the Arctic winter.

Right: *Hudson's Last Voyage* by artist John Collier. Hudson's crew mutinied and set him adrift in a small boat with his son John and seven other men but without food and fresh water.

Below: Greenlanders as seen by Sir Martin Frobisher in 1578. He brought an Inuit (eskimo) in 1578 back to London as proof of his voyage. Because this Inuit looked Asian, Frobisher wrongly believed that he had found the beginning of a strait that divided America from Asia.

In 1608 Champlain established a fur-trading post and then founded Quebec – the first permanent settlement in New France – on the St. Lawrence. Unfortunately, during the following harsh winter only 8 of the 24 settlers survived.

Champlain was friendly with the Algonquin and Huron Indians and joined their raids on the Iroquois tribes. In so doing, he became the first European to reach Lake Champlain – a lake that he named after himself. Between 1610 and 1626 he expanded Quebec and explored Ontario and Huron lakes.

When war broke out between England and France in 1626, the English fleet cut off supplies to Quebec and besieged the settlers for over a year. Quebec finally fell and Champlain was captured and taken to England. However, in 1632, the Treaty of Saint-Germain-en-Laye returned Quebec to France. Champlain sailed back to Canada, where he stayed until his death in 1635.

INTO THE INTERIOR

Much of America was still unexplored when, in 1665, Robert Cavelier sailed out to the French colonies in Canada. At first, he became a wealthy fur-trader near Montreal, but in 1673 he sold everything and set out to find the great rivers that the Indians had told him about. His expedition down the Mississippi began on 13th February 1682, reaching the Gulf of Mexico on 9th April. He claimed all the land drained by the Mississippi and its tributaries for France, calling the huge area Louisiana, after Louis XIV. In 1687, he was killed when some of his followers turned on him.

Another Frenchman, Jacques Marquette went as a missionary to the French province in New France. In May 1673 Marquette, François Jolliet, and five other men set out in canoes from St. Ignace across Lake Michigan, into the Fox River and across what is today Wisconsin. At the mouth of the Wisconsin River they saw the Mississippi and realized that it flowed into the Gulf of Mexico. Travelling back up the Mississippi to Illinois, they reached Lake Michigan. In 1674 Marquette set out from Green Bay, Wisconsin, to establish a mission in the area of Ottawa. He died there in 1675.

Below: Robert Cavelier, Sieur de La Salle, talking with Indians. He was a young trainee Jesuit priest who, like Marquette, knew a lot about Indian customs and took care to treat the Indian tribes with respect. Others who were less cautious were often killed by the Indians.

HUDSON BAY

Montreal

Mississippi River

LOUISIANA

Mississippi delta

Gulf of Mexico

Groseilliers

Cavelier

Left: Seventeenth-century explorations of the New World. Over the next century others were to build on the settlements of Cavelier and Marquette and push back the frontiers still further.

HUDSON BAY TRADERS

In 1670 a group of wealthy English merchants and noblemen, with the assistance of the French fur-traders Sieur des Groseilliers and Pierre Esprit Radisson, established the Hudson's Bay Company. Two years prior to this, Groseilliers had helped to direct a trading expedition to the Hudson Bay area. This was so successful that the English king, Charles II, gave the group a charter, establishing their sole trading rights in all the lands drained by the streams that flowed into the Hudson Bay. Over the next few years trading posts and forts were built all along the bay.

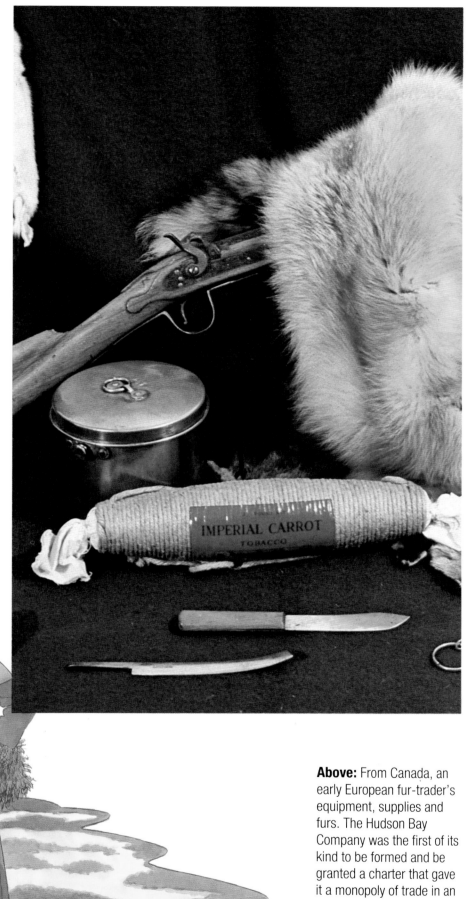

Above: From Canada, an early European fur-trader's equipment, supplies and furs. The Hudson Bay Company was the first of its kind to be formed and be granted a charter that gave it a monopoly of trade in an area of America. Although it began as a fur trader, it was soon selling a wide variety of other goods.

ABEL TASMAN

Dutch seaman Abel Tasman first went to sea as an ordinary sailor, but through hard work rose to be mate and then, within two years, master. By 1635 he was a *Commandeur*, a sort of admiral.

After distinguished service with The Dutch East India Company, Tasman came to the notice of Governor-General Van Diemen. He supported Tasman's project to sail further south in the Indian Ocean than anyone had gone before, so as to discover whether Australia reached down as far as the land mass of the Antarctic and was part of a giant southern continent.

On his most famous mission to the southern Pacific, in 1642–1643, Tasman made several discoveries. The first land that he reached was 500 km further south than the known coast of Australia. He called it Van Diemen's Land after his sponsor. Now it is called, more appropriately, Tasmania.

Amazingly, Tasman had sailed all round Australia but had not seen it. So he believed, but could not prove, that the "Great South Land", as it was known, was not connected to the polar continent. When Tasman left Van Diemen's Land a northwest wind blew him to the west coast of New Zealand, from where he went on to discover Tonga and Fiji.

In 1644 Tasman again set off to try to discover more about Van Diemen's Land, Australia and New Guinea. He found a passage into the Pacific Ocean north of Australia's Gulf of Carpenteria, and charted the western and northern coast up to the Torres Strait. In 1648, Tasman retired.

Above: Tasman sailed from Batavia with two ships, this one, the *Heemskerck*, and the *Zeehaen*, a warship but only lightly armed. When they reached Mauritius, they made repairs to the ships in preparation for the long voyage east to the southern lands.

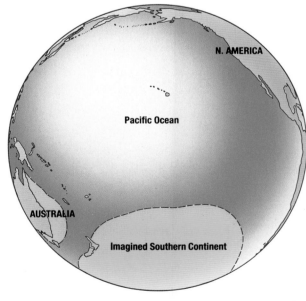

Above: From the days of the ancient Greeks until the voyages of seventeenth-century explorers such as Tasman, it was believed that a great continent lay to the south of Asia. The Greeks called it *Terra Australis* meaning Southern Land. Tasman mistakenly thought that western New Zealand was part of the southern continent.

Right: From Batavia, now known as Jakarta, in Java, Tasman's route followed a huge loop: to Mauritius east of Africa, down to the Antarctic (both outside of map area), across to Tasmania, on to New Zealand, north to Tonga and Fiji, and back to Batavia.

Below: Tasman in Tonga. When he reached Tonga and Fiji he was greeted with delight and stayed there for some time. He did not land in New Zealand as the native Maoris did not look friendly to him.

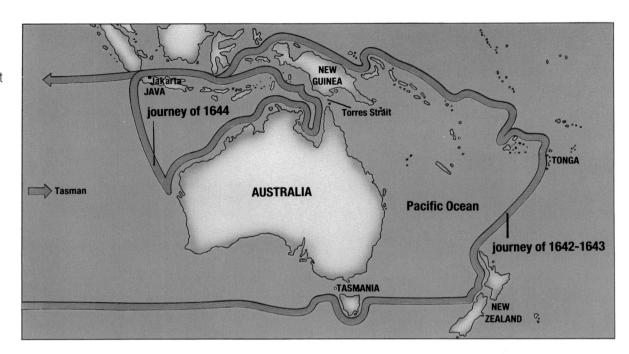

CAPTAIN JAMES COOK

James Cook was born in Britain on a Yorkshire sheep farm in 1728. As a young sailor, he distinguished himself by mapping the seas around Newfoundland, and as a reward was given command of an expedition to the South Seas. In 1768 Cook, with a crew of 85 and three scientists, set sail in *The Endeavour* to search for the legendary southern continent and to observe the planet Venus. He sailed round Cape Horn, reaching the Society Islands in the Pacific. Setting a course still farther to the west, he reached Australia and sailed along its east coast, claiming it for Britain. But the expedition was plagued with disease and returned to Britain three years after its departure, with only 50 men.

Cook's second voyage to the south began in 1772. From Cape Town, in South Africa, he sailed for 1,000 days, covering more than 120,000 km of the cold regions of the south. His ships were the first ever to cross the Antarctic Circle. And while he saw ice floes, he did not find the southern continent. He did not realize that he came within 120 km of Antarctica. Within a year of his return to Britain, he set sail again. This time, his mission was to try to find a northern outlet from the Pacific into the Atlantic Ocean. He rounded the Cape of Good Hope, went east to New Zealand, and then crossed the Pacific, sailing northwards along the shores of North America. Returning to the Sandwich (now Hawaiian) Islands, which he had discovered on his journey north, Cook was killed by the islanders while he was trying to retrieve a boat they had stolen.

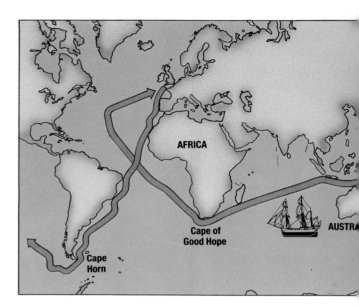

Right: During his voyage on *The Endeavour* Cook explored many new Pacific islands, claimed the east coast of Australia for Britain, and became the first person to cross the Antarctic Circle. Scientists travelling with Cook brought back many of the unusual animals they discovered. They were baffled by the fact that some animals, such as the kangaroo, existed in very few places.

Right: James Cook (1728–1779). He is remembered not only for his discoveries of new lands but also as the captain who eventually showed that eating fresh vegetables and drinking lemon juice could prevent scurvy, a disease caused by lack of vitamin C. On long voyages, fresh food would not keep so, until Cook's scheme, crews lacked vitamins.

Left: Although Cook encouraged his men to be friendly towards those whom they met in their travels around the islands, he himself was killed by natives in Hawaii when he returned there in 1779. The natives kept his body for several days then returned it, hacked to pieces, to the British. His remains were buried in Hawaii. This painting of the death of Cook is by British artist John Cleveley. It was based on a sketch of the incident by his brother, a carpenter on Cook's ship of the time, *The Resolution.*

ACROSS THE ROCKIES

During the eighteenth century many explorers were attracted to the huge land mass of North America. From 1731 to 1743, the French fur-trader, Pierre Gaultier de Varennes (Sieur de la Verendrye), and three of his sons explored as far west as present-day Saskatchewan. The Verendryes may have been the first Europeans to reach the Rocky Mountains.

In 1771, the English explorer Samuel Hearne proved that North America stretched to the Arctic. He explored the land between Hudson Bay and the Coppermine River, across the Northwest Territories in Canada. He was followed by Sir Alexander Mackenzie, a Canadian fur-trader, who in 1789 set off from Lake Athabasca to the Great Slave Lake. Exploring what is now known as the Mackenzie River, he found that the river led not to the Pacific, but to the Arctic.

A few years later, Mackenzie led an expedition up the Peace River through Alberta and into the Rocky Mountains. West of the mountains his party followed the Fraser River for about 160 km and then travelled overland to reach the Pacific. Mackenzie's journey proved that no waterway went as far as the Pacific coast. He reached his destination on 22nd July 1793, carving his name and the date on rocks at Cascade Inlet.

Mackenzie's example inspired other fur-traders to follow him. They included Simon Fraser and David Thompson of the North West Company, who between 1805 and 1811 started trading posts in the valley of the Fraser River (named after Fraser) and of the Columbia River.

Below: Exploration of the Northwest Passage in the late eighteenth century. Alexander Mackenzie found that the Mackenzie River flowed into the Arctic. David Thompson travelled along many waterways of the Northwest Territories.

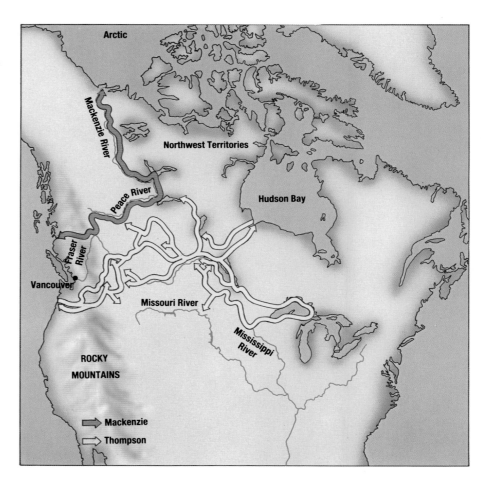

The site of the city of Vancouver was discovered by the Spaniard Juan Perez in 1774, and four years later Captain Cook landed at Nootka on the west of the nearby island. The island was named after Captain George Vancouver, who had been a mid-shipman on two of Cook's voyages.

In April 1791, following a dispute between British and Spanish ships off the North American coast, Vancouver was sent there to sort out the problems. He sailed via the Cape of Good Hope, Australia, and New Zealand. Having settled the dispute, he sailed round Vancouver Island and sighted the Strait of Georgia for the first time. He also surveyed the Pacific Coast north of San Francisco. On his return to Britain in 1795, he claimed both Vancouver Island and the mainland as British territory.

Above: Many explorers took with them people who decided to stay on in America to become trappers and hunters. It was a solitary and dangerous life. They would spend most of their time out in the wild, only returning to a fort to trade and buy essential provisions.

Right: A contemporary painting of an eighteenth-century Hudson Bay fur-trapper, his wife and dog.

LEWIS AND CLARK

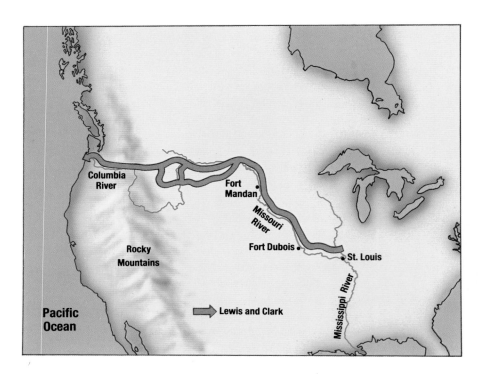

Above: Lewis and Clark travelled 13,000 km in an expedition that took two years to complete.

Below: On the second stage of the expedition Lewis and Clark used canoes. They were told by Indians that their big boats would be no good as the river became narrower and there were waterfalls ahead.

The Americans Meriwether Lewis and William Clark were the first explorers to have their expedition sponsored by a US president. President Thomas Jefferson chose Lewis to lead an expedition to open up the North frontier and find a land route to the Pacific coast. Lewis invited Clark, whom he knew from when they were in the army together, to accompany him.

In December 1803 the expedition party built Fort Dubois at the mouth of the Missouri River and there they constructed special boats 17 m long, that could be rowed, sailed, or poled like a raft. On 14th May 1804 they set off along the Missouri River. By October they had reached Fort Mandan, in North Dakota, where they stayed for the winter and were joined by a French Canadian trader Toussaint Charbonneau. The expedition

resumed in April 1805, using dugout canoes, as by now the river was too narrow for the boats.

On 26th May Lewis climbed to the top of a hill and caught his first glimpse of the Rocky Mountains that lay ahead. The next month was the hardest part of the journey, as the expedition crossed the mountains, often on dangerously narrow ledges. They eventually reached Clearwater River in Idaho. Here they built new canoes and paddled fast towards the Columbia River, reaching the Pacific coast before winter set in.

For the return journey they split up to try to find a shorter route over the Rockies. Lewis led a group directly east to the Missouri River. Clark almost retraced his steps, then followed the Yellowstone River to the Missouri. The two groups reunited in August 1806 and returned to St. Louis.

Above: A contemporary painting of one of Lewis's and Clark's canoes travelling down the Missouri River. On several occasions when they rested on the river bank, they had to fight off attacks not only by Indians but also by huge grizzly bears.

MUNGO PARK

Mungo Park was born in 1771 near Selkirk, in Scotland, where he studied to become a surgeon. However, it was his interest in botany that first brought him to the attention of the African Association, whose aim was to promote the exploration of Africa.

In 1795, the Association sent Park to explore the Niger River. He set off with two servants, one horse, and two donkeys, but on Christmas Day 1795 his party was attacked and robbed, and his servants fled. Undaunted, Park carried on, reaching the Niger River near present-day Segou, Mali, in June 1796. He followed its course a short way and saw that the river flowed eastward, not westward as other Europeans had thought.

Back in London in 1799, Park recounted all his adventures in his book *Travels in the Interior Districts of Africa*. He described how, on one occasion, he had been captured by a Moorish tribal chief but had managed to escape. For the next few years he returned to his native Scotland, where he worked as an ordinary country doctor.

Then, in 1805, the British Colonial Office asked Park to lead an expedition to trace the course of the Niger River. The expedition party set out from Gambia on the west coast of Africa. It consisted of about 40 European soldiers, carpenters, naval boat builders and surveyors, and an equal number of native helpers. However, it was badly organized so by the time it reached the Niger, there were only Park and 10 men left.

In November 1805 Park sent word to the Colonial Office that he was about to descend the Niger in a boat built by his men, which he named the Joliba, "the great water". Early in 1806, he sailed more than 1,600 km downstream to the Bussa rapids, now part of Kainji Lake in Nigeria, where it is believed that he drowned while trying to escape from an attack by African tribes.

After Mungo Park the European exploration of Africa reached its peak during the first half of the 1800s. In 1826, for example, the English explorer Alexander Gordon Laing travelled across the Sahara Desert from Tripoli in Libya, North Africa, to become the first European to reach the legendary city of Timbuktu on the Niger in present-day Mali.

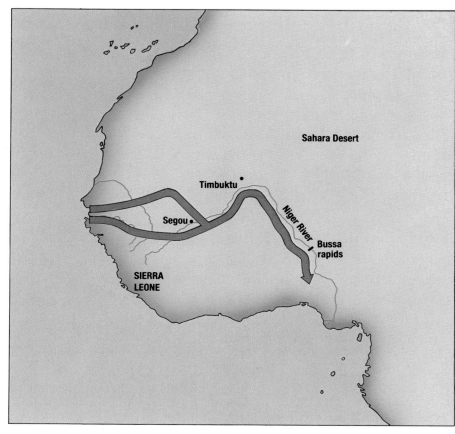

Right: Mungo Park made two expeditions to the Niger River. He took different routes to Segou, then followed the river south. In 1827, Frenchman René Caillié, inspired by Park's travels, set out from Sierra Leone for Timbuktu. He reached it the following year.

Left: For his second journey Park set off with a large party of native helpers. However, soon all but four of them had died of fever, or deserted.

Right: Mungo Park (1771-1806). Although he failed to reach the mouth of the Niger, he did establish its course. In the 50 years following his expeditions, French and German explorers mapped most of west Africa.

AROUND AUSTRALIA

Between 1798 and 1799, two British navigators, George Bass and Matthew Flinders, sailed around Tasmania to prove that it was an island.

Bass was an English surgeon turned explorer. In 1795 he travelled with Flinders a short way up the Georges River in southeast Australia, as far as where Sydney is today. Two years later Bass sailed south from Port Jackson (Sydney) to try to determine if Van Diemen's Land (Tasmania) was an extension of New South Wales. He sailed round to Western Port, through the strait now named after him, showing that the land discovered by Abel Tasman was very probably an island. The journey with Flinders finally proved that this was so.

Flinders then charted the Queensland coast. He completed the first circumnavigation of Australia in June 1803, finally proving that the mainland was a single huge land mass. In the course of his journey he met French navigator Nicolas Baudin, who was charting the coast from the opposite direction.

On his way back to England Flinders was shipwrecked off the island of Mauritius. He and his crew were rescued by the French, who controlled Mauritius, but they were immediately thrown into prison, as France was then at war with Britain. Flinders remained a captive for seven years, until 1810. Meanwhile Nicolas Baudin, on behalf of the French, had claimed all of Flinders' discoveries as his own. Only when Flinders published his book, *Voyage to Terra Australis*, shortly before his death in 1814, did he set the record straight.

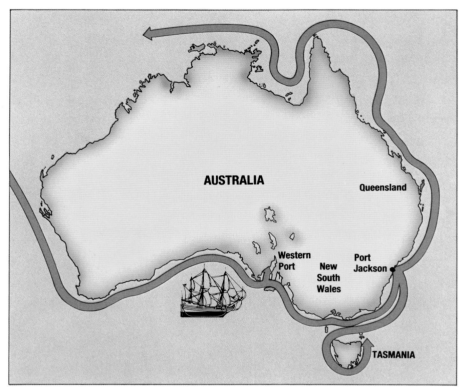

Above: The explorations of Bass and Flinders confirmed *Terra Australis* as the great southern continent. By the 1820s Australia had become its generally accepted name.

Left: A painting of Britain's Government House, Sydney, Australia, by William Westall, a landscape draughtsman on Flinder's expedition of 1802 to 1803.

Below: On his journey back to England in 1803, Flinder's ship, the *Porpoise*, ran aground on a reef. Soon after being rescued, he set sail again in a new ship, but this began to leak and he was forced to land on Mauritius, where he was imprisoned by the French for seven years.

THE NORTHWEST PASSAGE

The discovery of the Northwest Passage from Europe to the Far East, which led to the further exploration of the North American Arctic lands, was the achievement of Sir John Franklin.

Franklin was born in Lincolnshire, England, in April 1786. He joined the Royal Navy at the age of 15. A midshipman on Matthew Flinders' voyage around Australia in 1803, he displayed seamanship, courage, and resourcefulness and was later given command of an overland expedition from York factory, a trading post on Hudson Bay, to the Arctic. Between 1819 and 1822 he followed the Coppermine River and traced the shore line east of Coronation Gulf, covering 8,930 km. In a second expedition, a few years later, he sailed down the Mackenzie River to investigate the region west of the river's mouth. As a reward for his expeditions, he was knighted in 1829.

Franklin served as governor of Van Diemen's Land (Tasmania) until 1845, when he was sent to look for the Northwest Passage, a possible sea route around the north of Canada, linking the Atlantic and Pacific oceans. His ships, *Erebus* and *Terror*, were last seen in Baffin Bay around the 25th July 1845. After that, there was no further news of him or his expedition. More than 40 attempts were made to find him, but without success.

Right: The *Erebus* trapped in the ice. Although large and weighing 370 tonnes, *Erebus* and *Terror* could not get through. The men who tried to continue on foot over the ice floes were hampered by the heavy equipment they had to carry. It seems that Franklin and his crew died during 1848.

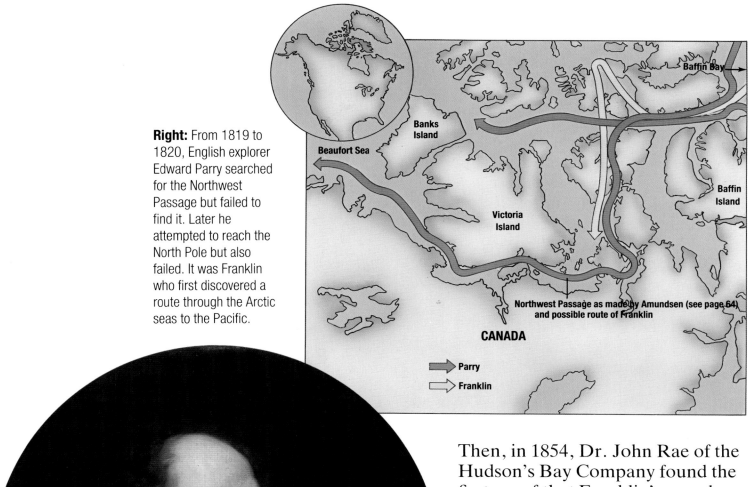

Right: From 1819 to 1820, English explorer Edward Parry searched for the Northwest Passage but failed to find it. Later he attempted to reach the North Pole but also failed. It was Franklin who first discovered a route through the Arctic seas to the Pacific.

Baffin Bay

Banks Island

Beaufort Sea

Baffin Island

Victoria Island

Northwest Passage as made by Amundsen (see page 64) and possible route of Franklin

CANADA

Parry

Franklin

Above: Sir John Franklin. When Franklin began his final Arctic journey he was almost 60 years old, and officially retired from Arctic exploration for nearly 20 years.

Then, in 1854, Dr. John Rae of the Hudson's Bay Company found the first proof that Franklin's vessels had sunk. In 1859, Leopold McClintock, on a trip sponsored by Lady Franklin, discovered a cairn or heap of stones on King William Island showing that Sir John had died on 11th June 1847, but had found the Northwest Passage.

The expeditions organized to search for Franklin led, partly by accident, to a thorough exploration of the Arctic region. One such search party, headed by the British explorer Sir Robert John McClure, discovered the Northwest Passage route. He sailed across the Beaufort Sea and around Banks Island, where his ship became stuck in the ice. He and his crew almost starved to death, before they were rescued in 1853. McClure then covered the rest of the Passage, travelling by ship and sled to Baffin Bay. On returning to England in 1854, in reward he was knighted.

THE SOURCE OF THE NILE

In 1858, two British explorers, Sir Richard Francis Burton and John Hanning Speke, became the first Europeans to see Lake Tanganyika, in Central Africa. Speke carried on separately to Lake Victoria, where, with J.A. Grant, he saw the mainstream of the Nile and decided to follow it.

Travelling downstream, Speke and Grant met Sir Samuel Baker, another British explorer, travelling in the opposite direction. Between them they charted the main part of the Nile. From 1861 to 1863 Burton returned to the Lake Victoria area and proved that here was the source of the Nile. Later, back in England, he published his book *The Lake Regions of Central Africa*.

Below: Two of Livingstone's African guides at Newstead Abbey, England, where he wrote a book about the Zambezi.

Right: Between them, Livingstone and Stanley opened up Central Africa and traced the course of the Congo.

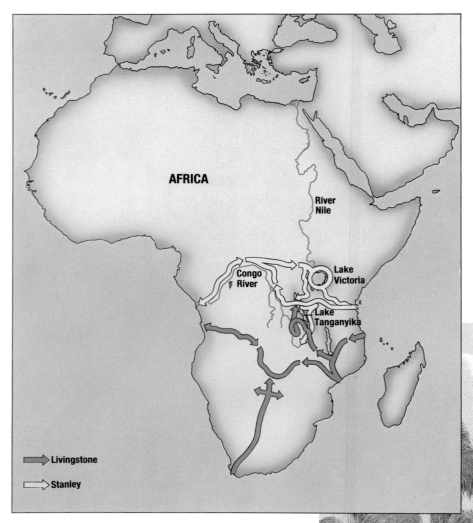

AFRICA

River Nile

Congo River

Lake Victoria

Lake Tanganyika

➡ Livingstone
⇨ Stanley

Below: Livingstone and Stanley travel together on a tributary of the Congo. It is hard to imagine what David Livingstone must have looked like after living for so long in Africa in primitive conditions, when Stanley arrived for their famous meeting on 10th November 1871. However, after nine months of hacking their way through 1,000 km of dense forest to reach him, Stanley and his companions were thrilled to see Livingstone.

LIVINGSTONE AND STANLEY

David Livingstone was a Scottish doctor and missionary who travelled across southern and southwest Africa from 1841 to 1856. After reaching Luanda, in present-day Angola, he journeyed eastward across the continent along the Zambezi River. From 1858 to 1863 he explored southeast Africa, reaching Lake Nyasa in Tanzania.

Livingstone explored east central Africa from 1866 until his death in 1873. At times, he seemed to be lost without trace, though he was, in fact, far in the interior carrying out the task he had set himself of being a missionary. It was during one of these periods that Henry Morton Stanley, a British reporter from the *New York Herald*, went to Africa to find him. Eventually, Stanley found Livingstone by Lake Tanganyika in 1871, greeting him with the words, "Doctor Livingstone I presume?"

In 1874, Stanley returned to Africa and succeeded in crossing the continent from east to west.

CHARLES DARWIN

Charles Darwin was one of the most influential figures of the 19th century, and a man who changed the course of human thinking. Born in Shrewsbury, England, in 1809, Darwin studied medicine at the University of Edinburgh and then theology at Cambridge University.

Between 1831 and 1836 he served as a naturalist on a British scientific expedition aboard HMS *Beagle*. The expedition visited places all over the world, allowing Darwin to study a huge variety of plants and animals. In South America he found fossils of extinct animals that closely resembled modern species, while on the Galapagos Islands, in the Pacific, he noticed that variations among plants and animals were similar to those he had seen in South America. Darwin returned to England in 1836 and spent the rest of his life studying specimens, doing experiments, and writing about his findings.

He devised important theories, based on his discoveries abroad, about how life on Earth had evolved. He published his findings in 1859 in a book called *On the Origin of Species*. There Darwin explained that animals had developed over millions of years into separate species through "natural selection": only animals suited to their environment would survive from generation to generation and produce young. This theory shocked most people of the day because it contradicted the religious view that each species had been created by a separate act of God. Today Darwin is judged to have been essentially correct.

Below: Darwin's studies of the finches on the Galapagos Islands led to his theories of evolution. He believed that the beaks of the finches varied from island to island as, over millions of years, one type of finch spread among the islands and adapted to the different plant foods available.

Left: Charles Darwin (1809-1882). His grandfather, Erasmus Darwin, was himself a naturalist and a contemporary of the great French naturalists, Jean-Baptiste de Lamarck (1744-1829) and Georges Cuvier (1769-1832), on whose work Charles Darwin developed his ideas of evolution. Even after his discoveries, Charles Darwin was reluctant to give up his religious faith. "Disbelief", he wrote, "crept over me at a very slow rate but was at last complete". Being forced to abandon his Christian faith made Darwin physically ill for years.

Below: Darwin's voyage on HMS *Beagle* took him round the world, but most notably to South America and to the Galapagos Islands, a group of 15 islands now belonging to Ecuador.

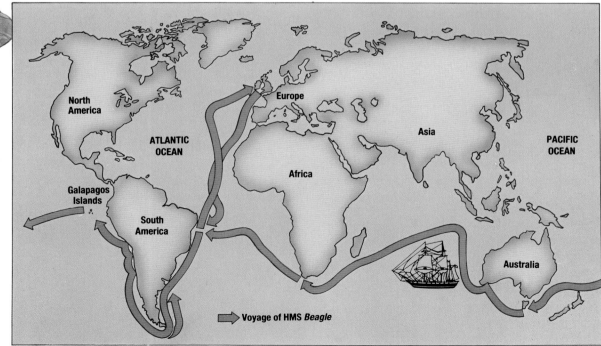

THE AUSTRALIAN INTERIOR

Until the nineteenth century most of inland Australia was still unexplored. It presented a major challenge because most of the area was a waterless desert.

In 1824 the English explorer Hamilton Hume and the Australian-born William Hovell, responded to the challenge. They opened up a route from Sydney – one of the earliest settlements in Australia – to the site of today's Melbourne. On their journey they sighted an exceptionally wide river.

Another Australian, Charles Sturt, was intrigued by their account of this river and decided to start his exploration there. He discovered the Darling River in 1828, and in 1829 commanded an expedition that went down the Murrumbidgee River on an old whaleboat. Sturt's party, almost by accident, entered the huge river seen by Hume and Hovell. Its strong current carried them straight down to its mouth, which they reached on 9th February 1830.

The return journey proved extremely hazardous. They had to travel against the current, food stocks were getting low, and when they reached the Murrumbidgee it was in full flood. At one time, they were also threatened by a huge crowd of Aborigines. The men rowed non-stop from dawn until dusk, with only an hour's rest at noon. By the time they reached Sydney, on 26th May 1830, they were exhausted and almost starving. They had travelled 3,000 km on the river that Sturt named the Murray.

Right: Aborigines – the native people of Australia – to this day manage to live in the interior, hunting wild animals and wandering in search of waterholes and shelter. Burke and Wills were wary of them and even refused their help when the two of them could have been saved from dying in the desert. This contemporary painting shows Aborigines confronting explorers in 1855, in Victoria.

Below: Burke and Wills' return journey to the south was a nightmare, as they struggled in soaring temperatures over deserted plains and scrub. Arriving in a desperate state at their intended supply camp they found that the group waiting for them with supplies had left that very morning. Three days after resuming their journey, both men had perished.

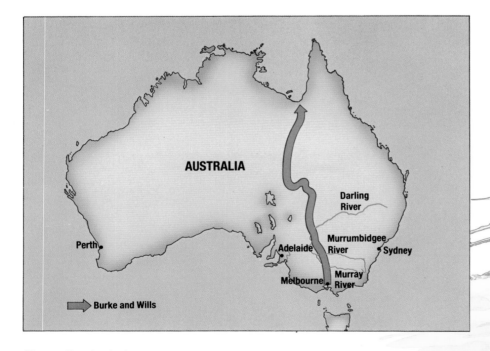

AUSTRALIA

Darling River

Murrumbidgee River

Perth

Adelaide

Sydney

Melbourne

Murray River

Burke and Wills

Above: Starting in August 1860, Burke and Wills took six months to make the first south to north crossing of Australia. By 1870 the numerous journeys of exploration across Australia had charted almost all of the territory.

The year before, a British sea captain, Charles Fremantle, landed on Australia's southwest coast and claimed the western part of the continent for Britain. Shortly afterwards, English settlers founded its capital, Perth.

In 1839 and 1840, Edward John Eyre became the first European to make a major overland journey across Australia from east to west. On his journey, he discovered the vast, dry salt lakes northwest of Adelaide, and the great lake now named after him.

When in 1860, the government of South Australia offered a prize of £2,000 to anyone crossing the continent from south to north and back again, Robert Burke and William Wills responded. With two others, they reached the northern coast, after incredible hardships in the deserts with temperatures of over 53°C. The return journey proved impossible to complete and they died of starvation.

WESTWARD HO!

From the late eighteenth century thousands of people left their homes on the eastern seaboard of North America and struggled west through narrow, steep trails over the Appalachian Mountains. This was the first great migration and the pioneers who made the journey became the first settlers in the west. Following the trail of the cattle raisers to the old frontier and beyond, they established new frontier settlements in Kentucky, Tennessee, Ohio, Illinois, and other places, as far west as the Mississippi River. They made clearings in the wilderness for small farms, and raised a few crops before moving farther west to look for the forests and fertile valleys they had heard about in the Oregon region and west of the Rockies.

The second great migration, in the wagon trains seen in "cowboy" films, brought settlers all the way to California and Oregon. There were many famous frontiersmen such as Davy Crockett, Kit Carson and Daniel Boone, who established the Wilderness Road through the old, narrow Cumberland Gap.

But the real heroes were the ordinary explorers who probably never thought of themselves as brave pioneers. Many of them were unhappy with their lives in the east and wanted the opportunity to start afresh. Some were escaping from religious persecution. In 1847, thousands of followers of the Mormon religion, led by Brigham Young, set off in wagon trains to seek new homes in the west. They finally settled near the Great Salt Lake in present-day Utah, and in 1851 began another settlement in the San Bernardino Valley.

Right: Early North American settlers migrated west in three main directions – to the forest lands beyond the Rockies, to the Great Plains, and to California.

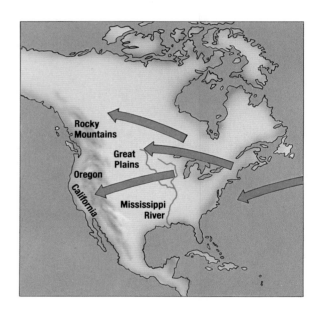

Left: Sam Brannan, the proprietor of a Mormon newspaper, wrote about California: "It (California) is a portion of the New World which God made choice above all others." Little wonder then that so many wagon trains like these went west!

Above: Emigrants moving with a covered wagon into Loup Valley, Nebraska, in 1886. Like many heading west, they hoped to escape from the diseases that were found in the first settlements in the Mississippi valley and in the eastern towns.

61

ACROSS THE GOBI

The explorer Sir Francis Edward Younghusband was a British Army officer who travelled all over Burma, Manchuria, and the Gobi and Taklamakan deserts.

When he was 24, he was given the opportunity to travel back from China to central Asia, across the Gobi Desert – a journey which no European had ever done before. The expedition set out on 4th April 1887, and 10 days later reached the open plain of Mongolia. Once in the desert, the routine they followed never varied. In the mornings, Younghusband kept his diary up to date. Then, to avoid the worst of the heat, they would set off on their camels after 3 p.m. and carry on until midnight or later, often guided only by the light of the stars. It took them 70 days to complete the journey of more than 2,000 km across the desert.

Early in the 20th century the British Viceroy of India, Lord Curzon, sent Younghusband to Tibet. His task was to counter the growing Russian and Chinese influences there and to force the Tibetan leader, the Dalai Lama, to come to an agreement with Britain. He was accompanied by 3,000 Indian soldiers and 10,000 others. After a clash, in 1903, with 2,000 Tibetan soldiers, Younghusband arrived in Lhasa in August 1904. It was the first time for over 50 years that any European had entered the holy city. By then, however, the Dalai Lama had fled to China and though an agreement was signed between Tibet and Britain, it was of little use as Tibet came increasingly under Chinese influence. Today, it is part of China.

Below: Younghusband and his guides trek across the plain of Mongolia before obtaining camels and crossing the Gobi. So silent was the desert that he described the hum of insects and noises of the birds at an oasis as "deafening".

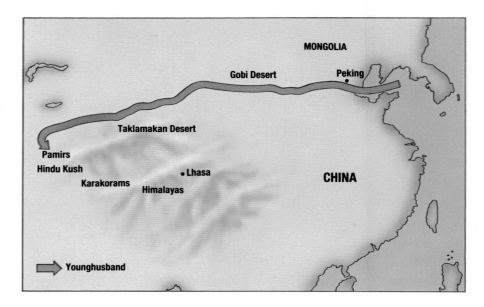

Above: From 1889 to 1895 Younghusband made many surveying and exploration journeys among the Karakoram, Pamir and Hindu Kush mountains – the kind of terrain he had known from his boyhood. In later life, he became an active supporter of British expeditions to climb the high peaks of the Himalayas.

Right: To this day, peoples of the Gobi Desert such as these wander with their camels to trade at markets and to find water and grazing areas.

RACE TO THE POLES

From the late 1890s a US civil engineer, Robert Edwin Peary, tried again and again to reach the North Pole, but without success. Then, at the age of 52, he set out once more and, on 6th April 1909, eventually reached the Pole.

When he heard of Peary's success, the Norwegian explorer Roald Amundsen decided to conquer the South Pole. So too did the British Captain Robert Falcon Scott. Amundsen set out from Norway in June 1910 – Scott left England at the same time.

From January to October 1911 Amundsen's crew made short journeys into Antarctica setting up stores of food and fuel. With the coming of the Southern spring, on 19th October 1911, Amundsen and his crew set off for the Pole in four sleds pulled by 52 Eskimo dogs.

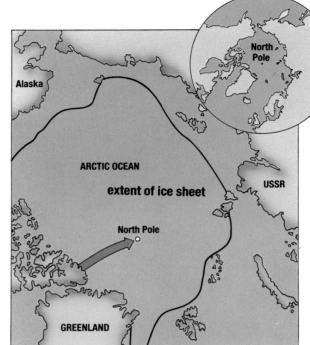

Left: In autumn 1908, Peary and his team set out for the North Pole from the northwest coast of Greenland with 49 Inuit (Eskimo) helpers and 246 dogs on board his ship, the *Roosevelt*. He left the ship on 22nd February 1909 and made the 650 km journey to the Pole.

Below: Peary after his return from the North Pole to his base camp in 1909. In 1898 he had got to within 630 km of the Pole, and in 1905 to within 320 km.

Scott used ponies instead of dogs. But after a few days the ponies became exhausted and had to be shot, and the men had to pull the sleds instead. Scott had chosen the wrong clothing too, and the route he followed was longer and more difficult than Amundsen's.

On 14th December 1911 Amundsen reached the Pole. Three days later he began the return journey, leaving a tent and a Norwegian flag behind to mark his triumph. It was these that the disappointed Scott found when he reached the Pole five weeks later on 17th January 1912.

On their return trip all five members of Scott's party died from hunger, cold, and exposure. The diaries they kept with details of their epic journey were found with their bodies months later.

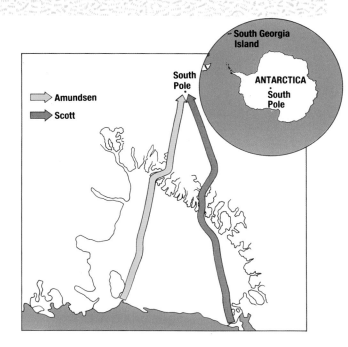

Right: In the autumn of 1910, while in Melbourne, Australia, Scott received a message from Amundsen – the race to the South Pole was on! Amundsen won, and Scott's party never returned home. They died just 14 km from a store of food and fuel.

Below: Two of Amundsen's party at the South Pole, December 1911. In 1908 Sir Ernest Henry Shackleton, an Irish explorer, led a British expedition to within 156 km of the South Pole. In 1914, he led an expedition into waters to the west of Antarctica where ice closed in and crushed his ship. His party escaped in boats to South Georgia Island and alerted his rescuers from its summit.

FIRST FLIGHT

The first powered flight took place on 17th December 1903. It was the result of years of planning, and trying and failing on the part of two gifted and determined brothers, Wilbur and Orville Wright. Wilbur was born on 16th April 1867 and Orville four years later. From early childhood, the brothers always had ambitions to start something new. In 1889 they started a newspaper, but the project failed after a few months. Three years later they opened a bicycle shop, and soon were making their own bicycles. In 1899 they made a biplane kite to test ideas they had about flying.

Finally, in 1903, they succeeded in making the world's first powered flight, over a distance of 252 m. Their third plane, built in 1905, flew over 38 km in 38 minutes. The Wrights had begun a new age of powered flight and soon began to sell their aircraft. But in 1912 Wilbur Wright died of typhoid and Orville felt unable to carry on alone, so sold the business in 1915.

On 25th July 1909 a light monoplane, developed from the Wrights' idea, and piloted by Louis Blériot, a Frenchman, flew from a cliff top near Calais 34 km across the English Channel to Dover. Blériot's plane had an engine and propeller at the front, to "pull" the aircraft along, which was a great improvement over the "pusher" engines of the Wrights.

The first great long-distance flight took place on 14-15th June 1919, when two Britons, Captain John Alcock and Lieutenant Arthur Whitten Brown flew 3,000 km non-stop across the Atlantic from Newfoundland to Ireland.

Below: Amy Johnson, a British aviator who broke many speed-flying records, flies over the Indian countryside on her way to achieving the world's first solo flight by a woman from England to Australia in 1930.

Above: Alcock and Brown land their aircraft in a bog at Clifden, Ireland, after the first Atlantic plane-crossing in 1919.

Below: Charles Lindbergh an American aviator, with the *Spirit of St. Louis*, in which he made the first non-stop solo flight across the Atlantic in 1927.

UNDER THE SEA

I n 1872 the first oceanic investigation took place, led by the Scottish naturalist Charles Wyville Thomson in his ship *Challenger*. He and his team spent three years at sea, travelling more than 110,000 km. The expedition made over 350 stops to take soundings (measure water depths) and to collect specimens of underwater life. The 50-volume report they wrote on their return established the new science of oceanography.

Some 70 years later, the Swiss inventor Auguste Piccard made a major contribution to ocean exploration by inventing a diving vessel called a bathyscaphe. In 1960 his son Jacques, and Lieutenant Don Walsh of the US Navy, dived in the bathyscaphe *Trieste* into the Mariana Trench, a valley in the ocean floor off Guam in the Pacific Ocean, known to be the deepest place in the world. They descended 10,910 m, reaching to within about 120 m from the bottom.

In 1969 Jacques and a crew of five drifted on the Gulf Stream from Palm Beach, Florida, to Cape Cod, Massachusetts, in a specially built craft, the *Ben Franklin*. The expedition collected valuable information about currents and drift, and also helped NASA, the US space agency, to investigate human reactions to several days confinement in cramped spaces for future space programmes.

Jacques-Yves Cousteau, a French oceanographer, author and film producer, developed many special techniques for undersea exploration. In 1943, Cousteau helped invent the aqualung. This breathing device enables a diver to move about freely under water for long periods. Cousteau also developed the first underwater diving station and an observation vehicle called the "diving saucer". Since 1951, he has continued to explore the oceans on his research ship *Calypso*, and has made many underwater documentary films.

Left: Jacques-Yves Cousteau, seen here with his team (he is on the far left) and a submersible, has been concerned with protecting as well as exploring the marine world. In the 1960s and 1970s, his popular television series "The Undersea World of Jacques Cousteau" was seen all over the world. It showed people the excitement, wonder, and dangers of being a discoverer under the sea, and emphasized how important it was to preserve marine life.

Above: A diver explores underwater wildlife, relying on the aqualung she wears on her back for a constant supply of fresh air. An aqualung is often called a scuba, short for self-contained underwater breathing apparatus.

Right: The US manned Deep Submergence Research Vehicle *Alvin* makes another dive to depths of 4,000 m to explore the sea bed and search for wrecks. It has cameras and lights, remote-controlled "arms" and many recording instruments.

ON TOP OF THE WORLD

In 1858 the Surveyor General of India for the British Government, Sir George Everest, plotted on paper for the first time the highest mountain in the world, at 8,839 m. It was in the Himalayan range between India and Tibet and it has carried his name ever since.

Mt. Everest became the ultimate challenge for every mountaineer. But not until 1921 did the Tibetan government give permission for an Everest climb. The first attempt was made by C.K. Howard-Bury. His team managed, without oxygen masks, to climb to 8,230 m.

Above: Because of its commanding size and height, Everest was known in the native Tibetan language as Chomolungma – "Goddess Mother of the World". The summit reaches two-thirds of the way through the Earth's atmosphere to where there is little oxygen and it is extremely cold and windy.

Left: Hillary and Tensing prepare for their assault on the main summit of Everest. To reach this point, they had escaped falling into crevasses, being swept downhill by avalanches, and tumbling down rockfaces.

Right: Tensing photographed by Hillary on Everest's summit. His ice-axe carries the flags of Nepal, India, the UK and the United Nations. Tensing, a Buddhist, offered food to the gods; Hillary laid a crucifix in the snow. After 15 minutes they began their descent.

In 1924 two climbers, Norton and Somervell, were just 300 m from the top when they had to turn back. Two of their companions, Mallory and Irvine, vanished completely after having last been seen pushing on towards the summit. Mallory's ice-axe was later found some way below the summit by the 1933 expedition, which reached the same spot as Norton and Somervell had done before giving up.

In 1953 Sir John Hunt led a further expedition to Everest. Hunt set up a series of camps, gradually moving towards the peak. On the 27th May two of the party, Bourdillon and Evans, reached the south summit at 8,745 m. Two days later, starting from a camp at 8,500 m, Sir Edmund Hillary and Tensing Norgay made the final ascent to the top. At 11.30 a.m. on 29th May, the two men were literally "on top of the world".

SOLO ROUND THE WORLD

Below: Solo yacht racing, which brought many recent adventurers round-the-world sailing fame, is exciting, hard work, and, during storms like this, terrifying.

The first person to sail single-handed around the world was Francis Charles Chichester. Born in 1901 in Shirwell, England, as a young man he went to New Zealand, where he spent 10 years working as a sheep farmer, coalminer, and prospector.

In 1929 Chichester flew solo from England to Australia in a Gypsy Moth biplane, and two years later made the first east-west flight across the Tasman Sea between New Zealand and Australia. He also won the first solo transatlantic sailing competition in 1960, and later broke his own sailing speed records several times.

He made his famous round-the-world solo voyage in 1966–1967 on board the 16.2 m ketch, *Gypsy Moth IV* – a feat for which he was knighted. The Sydney (Australia) to Plymouth (England) leg of that trip, which covered 24,972 km, was the longest non-stop voyage ever made in a small sailing ship.

OTHERS GO IT ALONE

Alec Rose was born in Canterbury, England in 1908. He served in the Royal Navy in World War II, and later developed the ambition to sail single-handed around the world. On his first attempt, in 1966, his yacht, *Lively Lady*, was so badly damaged that after only a few days at sea he had to return and start again. Setting out again a year later, he reached Melbourne, Australia, and then set off for Cape Horn. But further damage to his yacht forced him to put in at New Zealand before carrying on. The return journey to England lasted five months, during which Rose faced great difficulties and danger.

The British yachtswoman Clare Mary Francis was the first woman to sail solo round the world, in the Whitbread Round-the-World Race in 1977-1978. She had twice earlier been the first woman home in transatlantic single-handed races, in 1973, and again in 1976, when she established the women's world solo record, which is still unmatched.

Below: Francis Chichester coiling rope on Gypsy Moth IV. The photo was taken by a remote control camera.

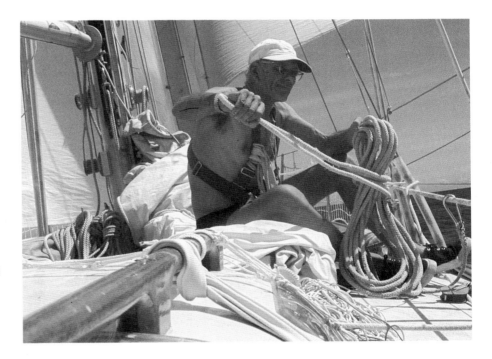

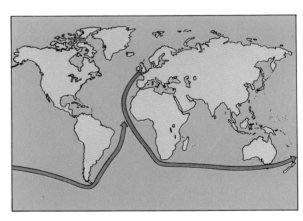

Above: For his world solo voyage, Francis Chichester set sail on 27th August 1966 and reached home again on 28th May 1967. He had sailed 47,360 km via the southern tips of Africa, Australia and America.

INTO SPACE

The final frontier of exploration – outer space – was reached on 4th October 1957, when the USSR put the unmanned satellite *Sputnik 1* into orbit around the Earth. On 12th April 1961 the Soviet cosmonaut Yuri Gagarin became the first person to orbit the Earth, in his spaceship *Vostok 1*. When, on 5th May Alan Shepard became the first American to do the same, this signalled that the USA had entered the "space race".

Two years later US President Kennedy committed the USA to putting a person on the Moon before the end of the 1960s. Eventually, at 2.32 p.m. GMT on Wednesday 16th July 1969, Apollo 11 set off for the Moon. On board were Neil Armstrong, Edwin "Buzz" Aldrin, and Michael Collins. On 19th July they were orbiting the Moon, and the following day, at 6.47 in the evening, the lunar module *Eagle*

swung clear of the mother ship *Columbia* and descended to the Moon's surface.

Early on the morning of Monday 21st July, Neil Armstrong climbed down the ladder onto the Moon itself. Edwin Aldrin joined him minutes later. The astronauts returned safely to Earth. Their journey opened a new chapter in exploration.

Below: During the 2½ hours that they spent on the Moon, Armstrong and Aldrin collected rock samples and planted a flag. Later astronauts used Moon buggies like this. One astronaut even played golf!

Right: Apollo 11 landed near the centre of the side of the Moon visible from Earth. Altogether, there have been more than 20 lunar landings, but only six of them manned, and all by US astronauts.

Right: A painting of US *Voyager 2* spaceship on its way past the planet Uranus. A new frontier is now ready for exploration. In 1990 a second US President set a deadline for exploring space. President Bush has pledged that the USA will put an astronaut on Mars within the next 30 years. This will almost certainly happen.

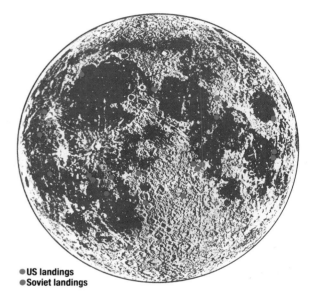

● **US landings**
● **Soviet landings**

INDEX

ACKNOWLEDGEMENTS
All maps by Hayward Art Group.

Artwork as follows: Nick Hewetson pages 8-9, 10-11, 14-15, 20-21, 26-27, 35, 38-39, 46-47, 56-57, 72. Mark Bergin pages 12, 30-31, 40, 60-61, 66-67. John James pages 16-17, 22-23, 24-25, 28-29, 32-33, 44-45, 48, 50-51, 52-53, 58-59, 62-63.

Photographs as follows (t=top, b=bottom, l=left, r=right): 9, 10, 13 Michael Holford. 15 Canadian Park Service. 16 The Bodleian Library, University of Oxford (shelf number: B1439). 18 Bibliotheque Nationale, Paris. 18-19 Edinburgh University Library. 21 Michael Holford. 23 e.t. archive. 25 Mary Evans Picture Library/Explorer. 26 National Maritime Museum. 28-29 Mary Evans Picture Library. 32, 34 By courtesy of the National Portrait Gallery, London. 35 British Museum. 36-37 The Hulton Deutsch Collection. 37 Tate Gallery, London. 39 National Film Board of Canada. 41 Mary Evans Picture Library. 42-43 Michael Holford. 43 National Maritime Museum. 45 Hudson Bay Company. 47 National Film Board of Canada. 49 National Portrait Gallery, London. 50-51 Royal Commonwealth Society, London. 54 Royal Geographical Society, London. 55 Mary Evans Picture Library. 57 Ann Ronan Picture Library. 59 The Hutchison Library. 61 The Hulton-Deutsch Collection/ The Bettmann Archive. 63 J. Bitsch/Zefa. 64 The Hulton-Deutsch Collection. 65, 67t, 67b Mary Evans Picture Library. 68 Planet Earth Pictures/Flip Schulke. 69t Armstrong/Zefa. 69b Woods Hole Oceanographic Institution. 70 Royal Geographical Society, London. 70-71 GSF Picture Library. 71 Royal Geographical Society, London. 73 Francis Chichester Limited. 74 NASA. 75 Julian Baum.